Drawing Birds: How To Draw A Bird For Beginners

How To Draw Birds Step By Step Guided Book

By Gala Publication

Published By:

Gala Publication

ISBN-13: 978-1515168713
ISBN-10: 1515168719

©Copyright 2015 – Gala Publication

Table of Contents

Canary

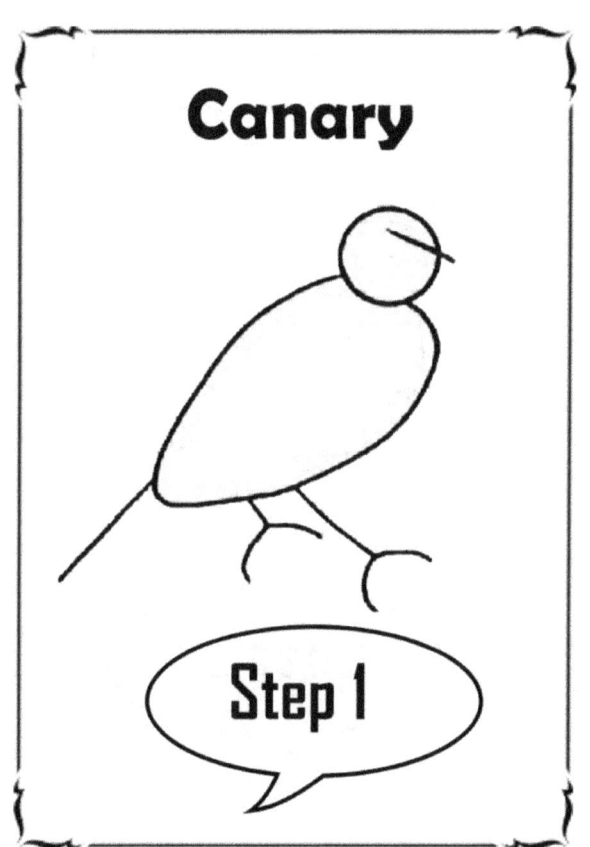

Step 1

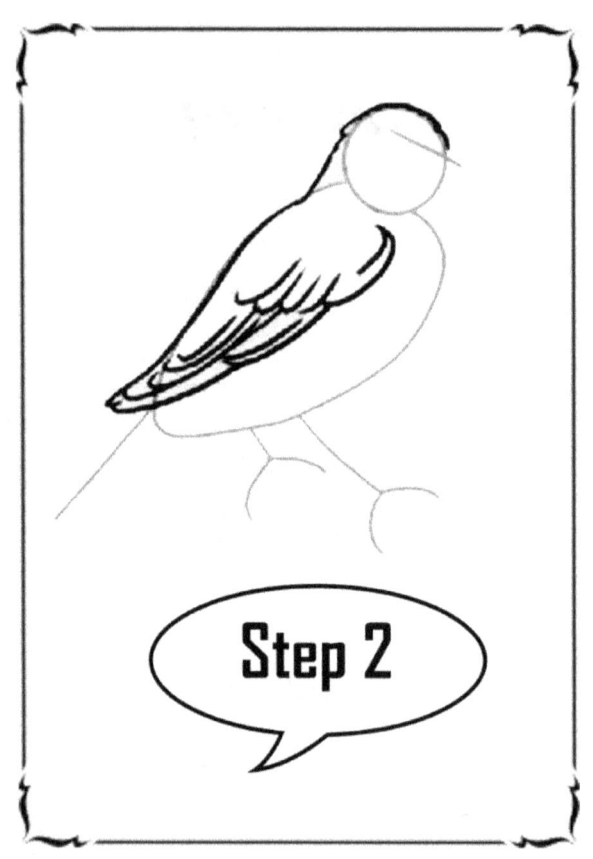

Step 2

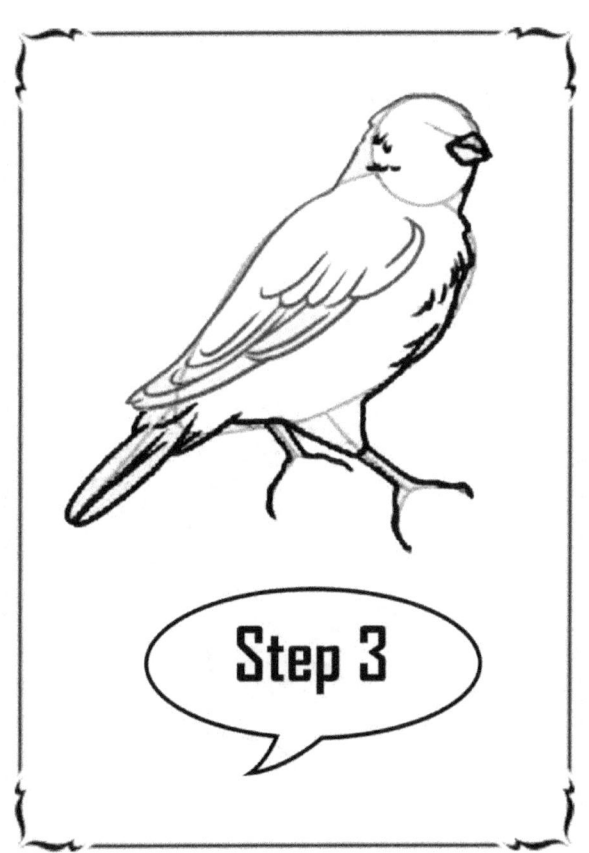

Step 3

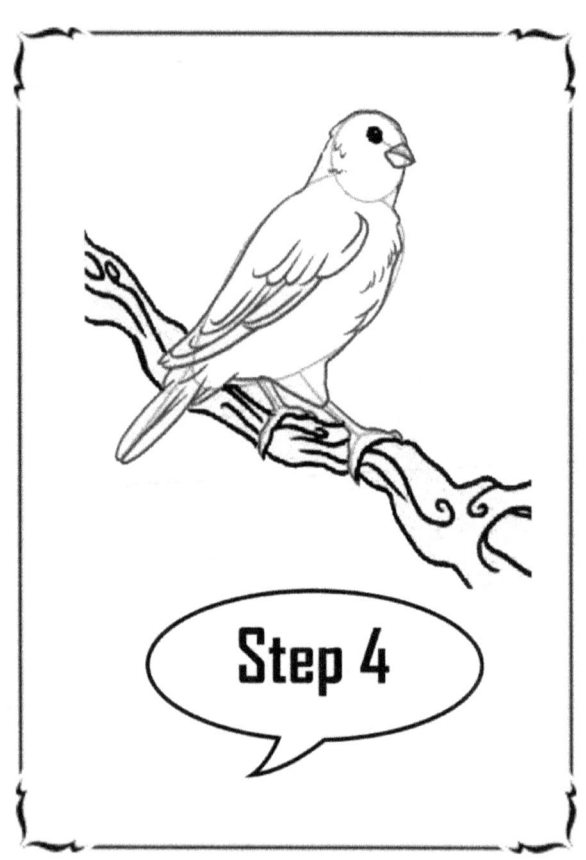

Step 4

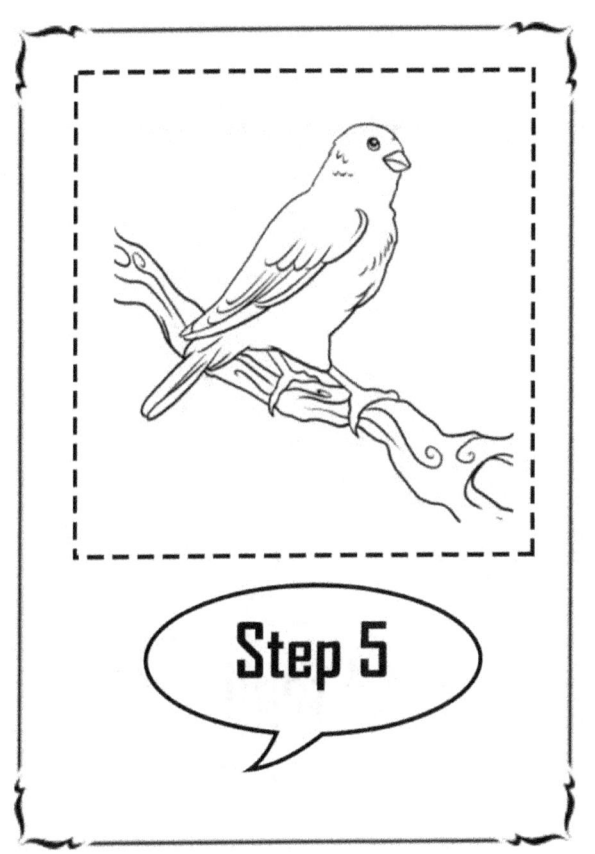

Step 5

Cardinal

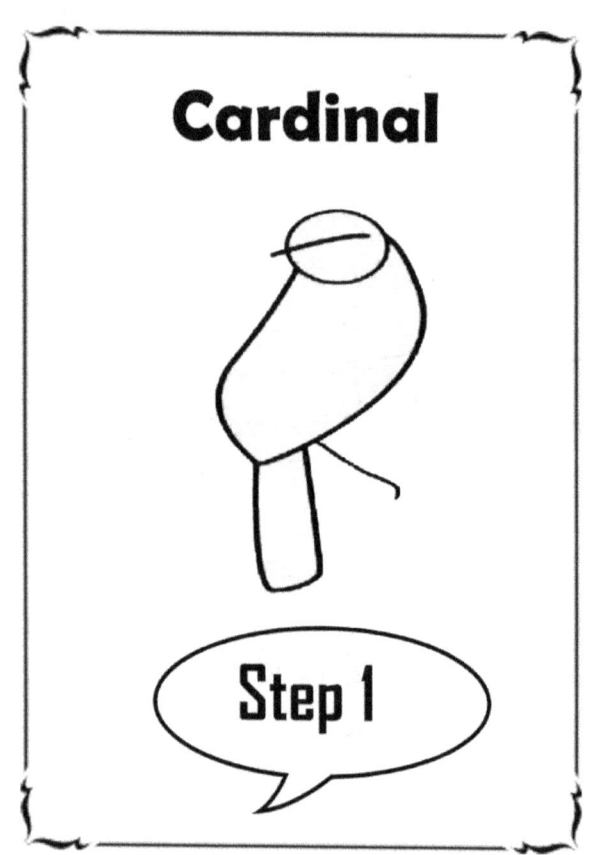

Step 1

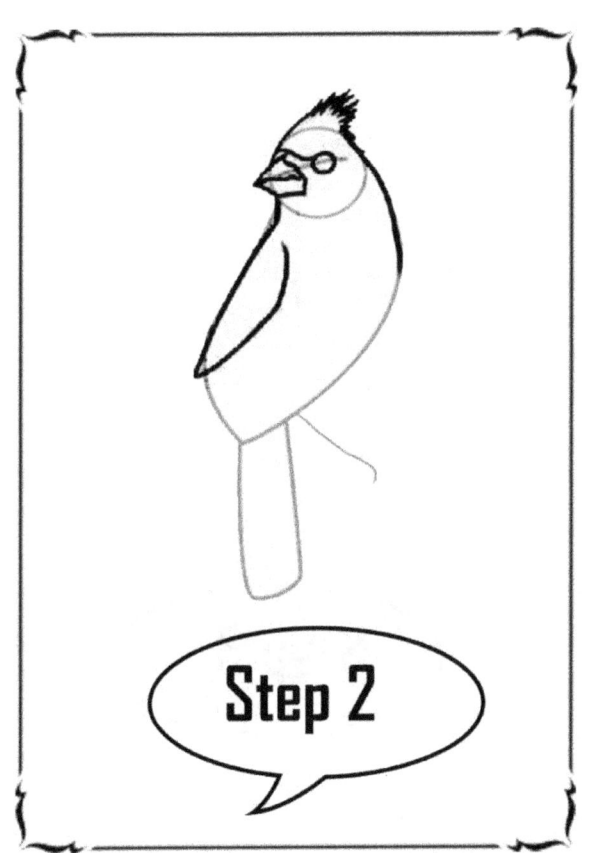

Step 2

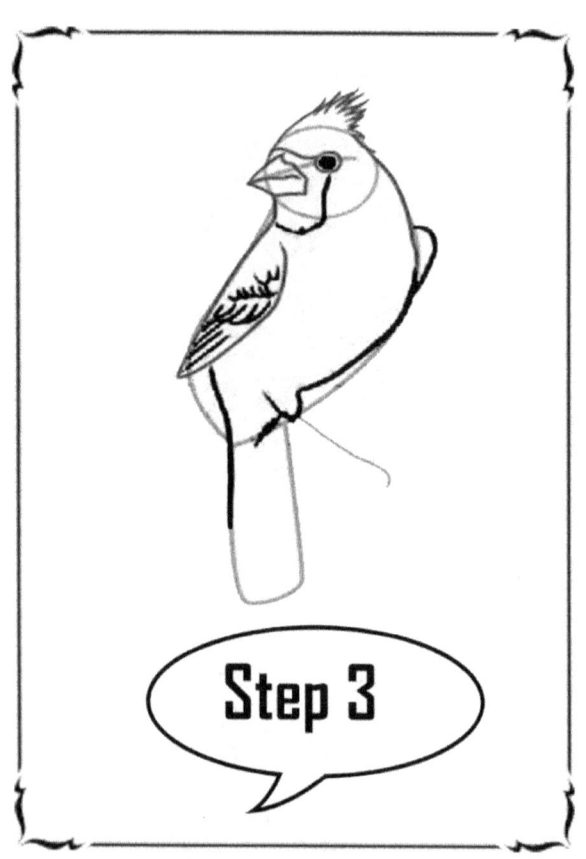

Step 3

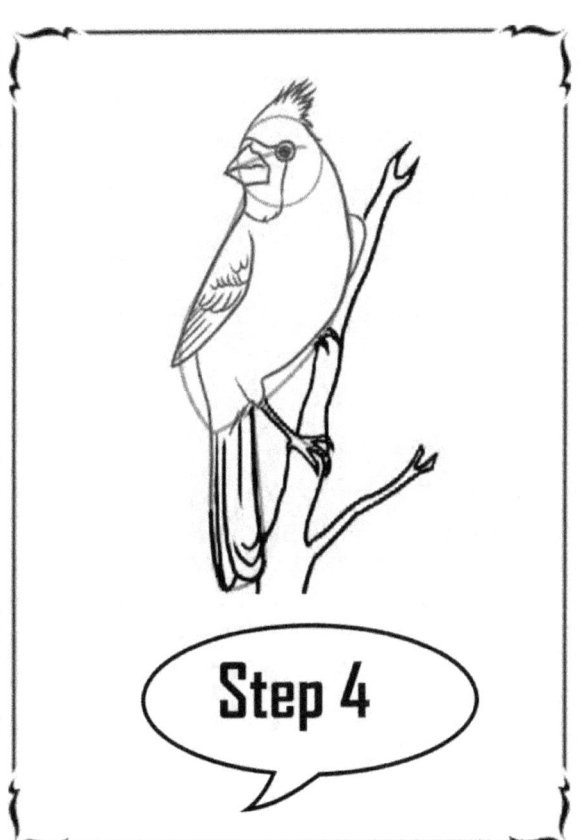

Step 4

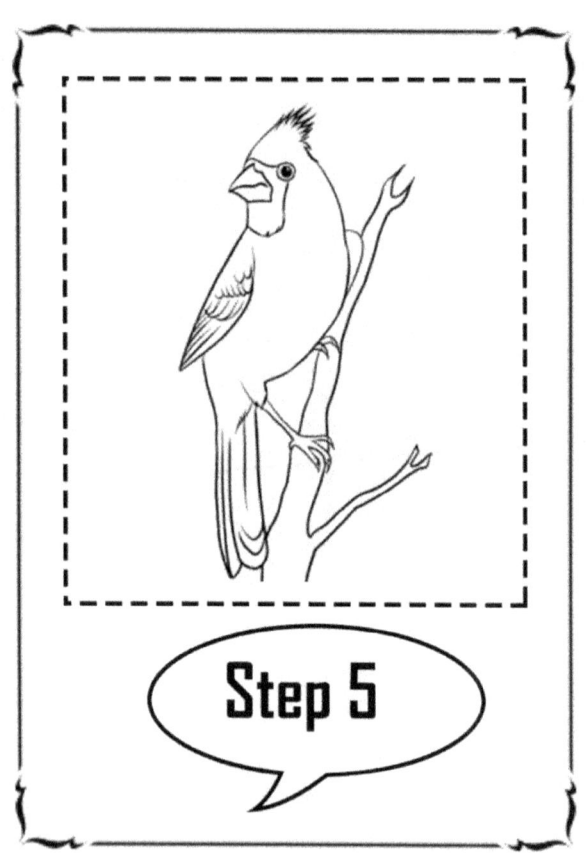

Step 5

Mockingbird

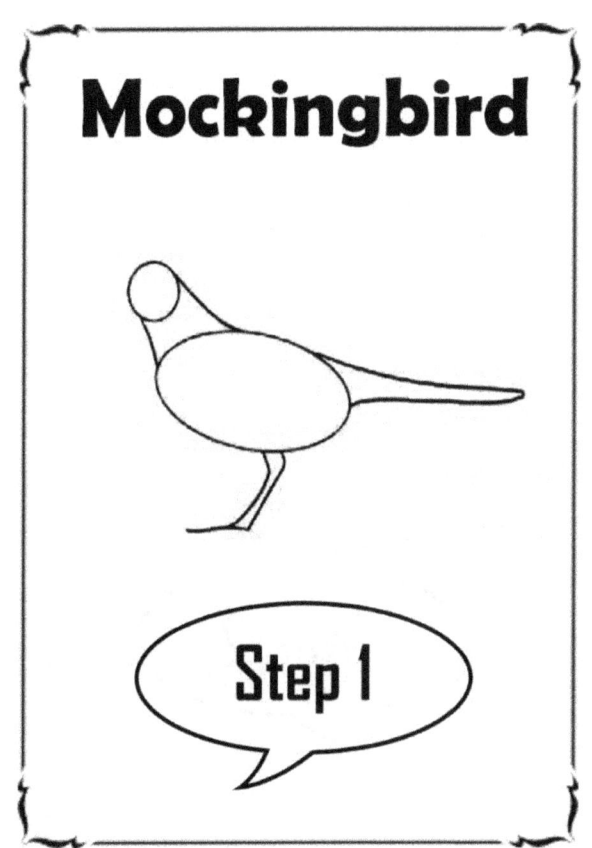

Step 1

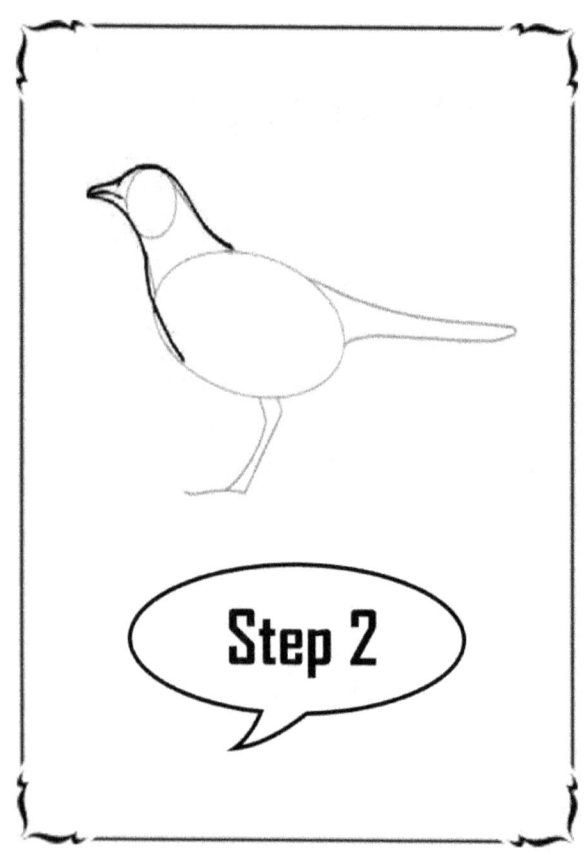

Step 2

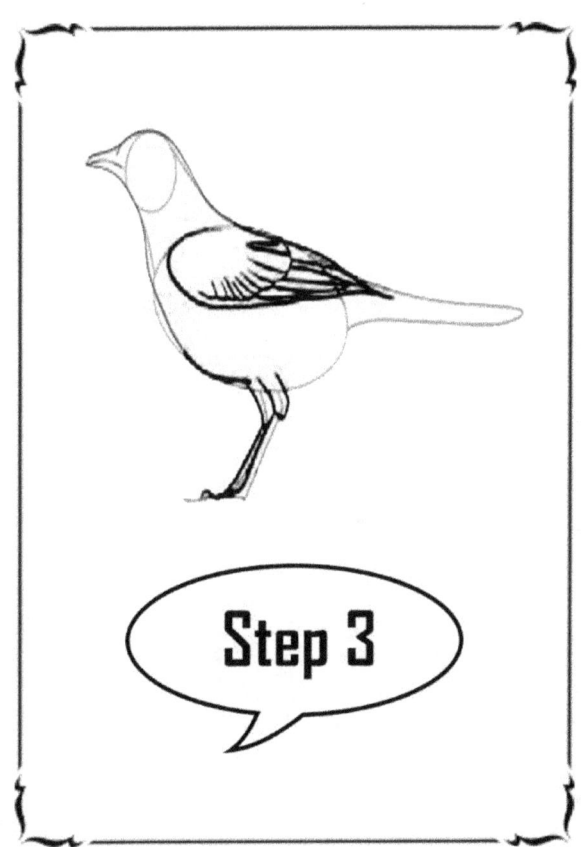

Step 3

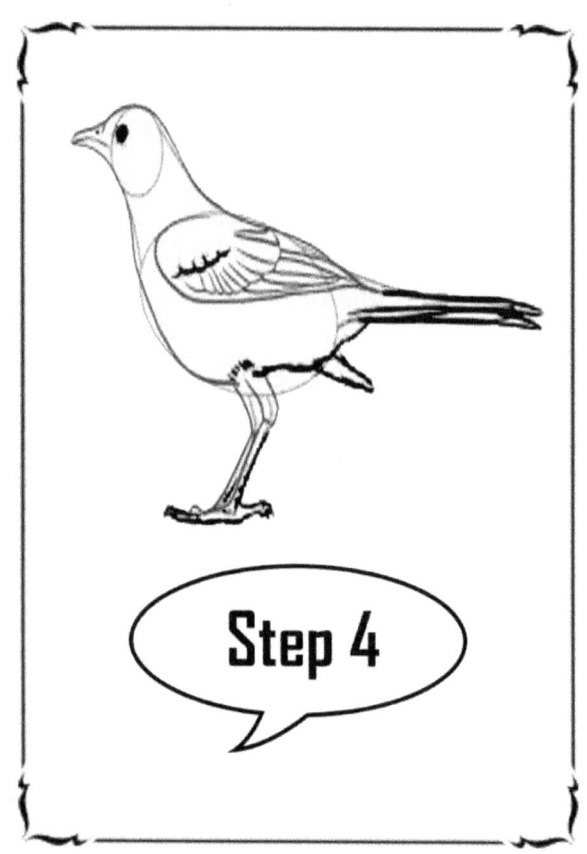

Step 4

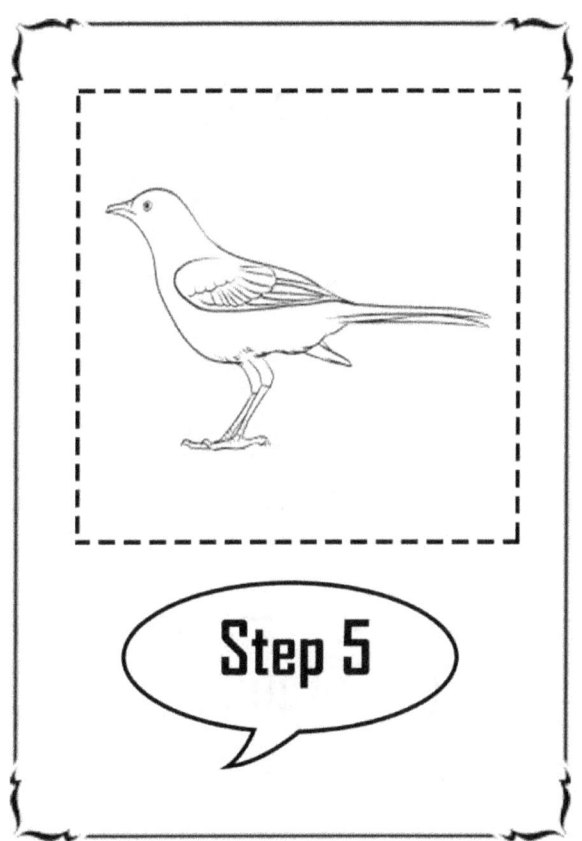

Step 5

Finch

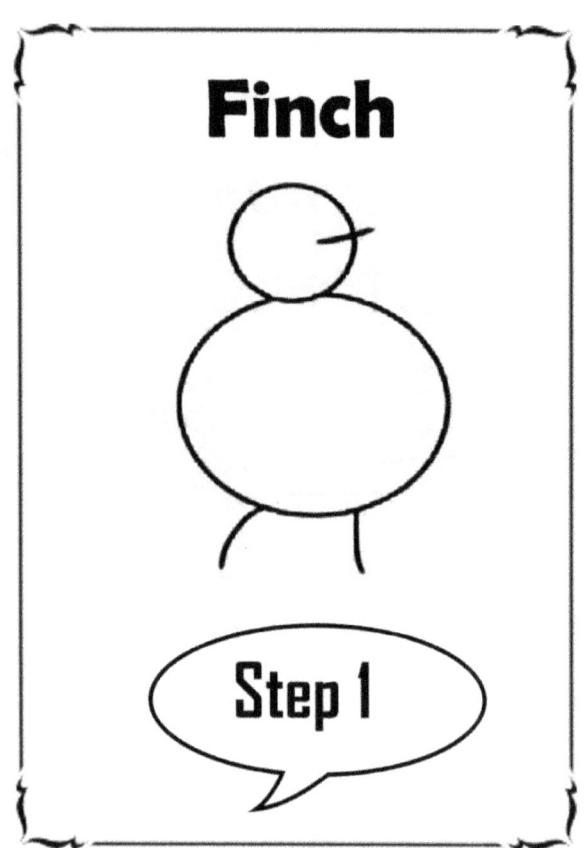

Step 1

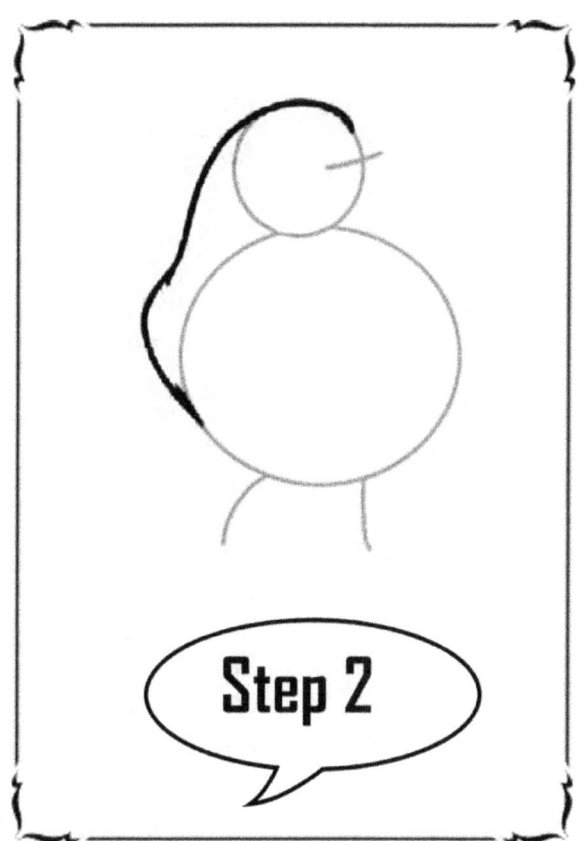

Step 2

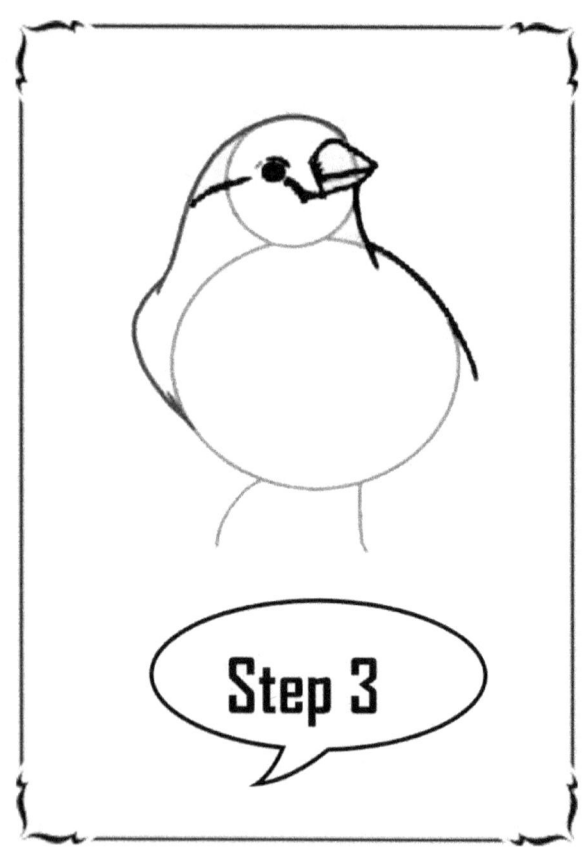

Step 3

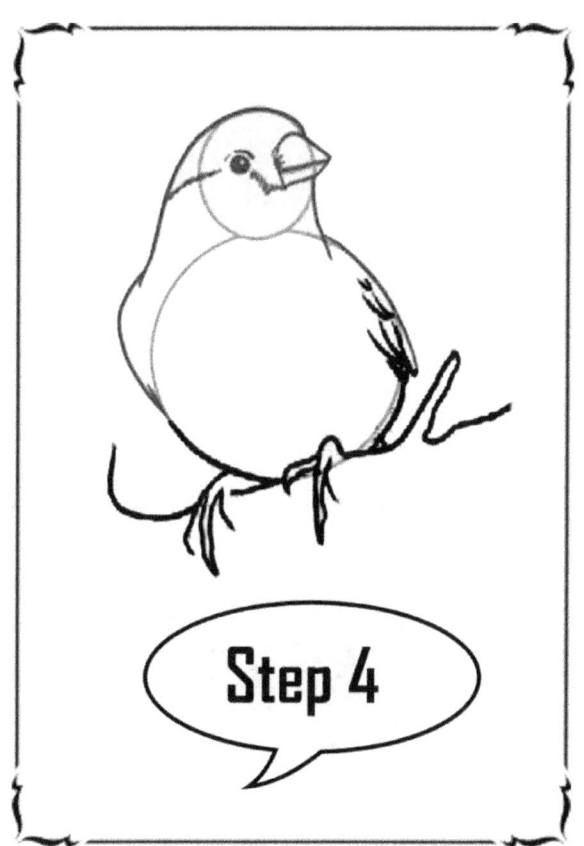

Step 4

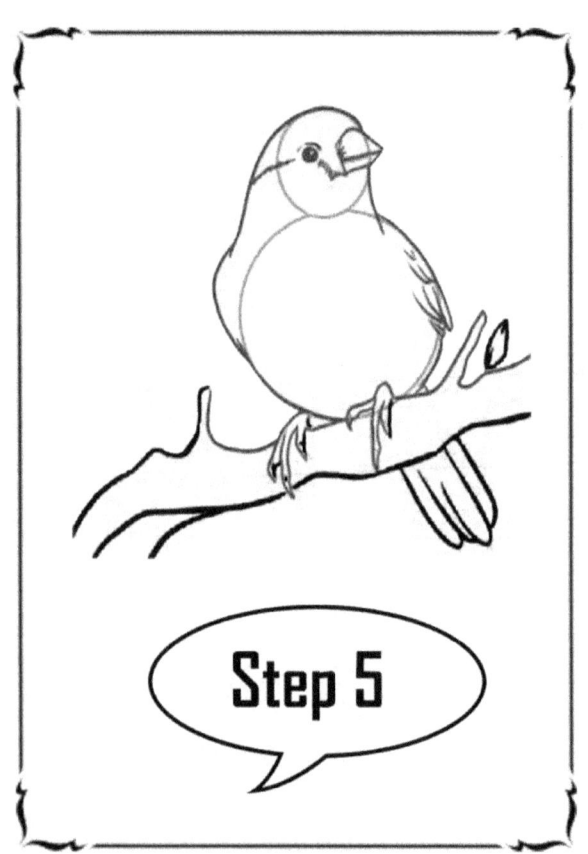

Step 5

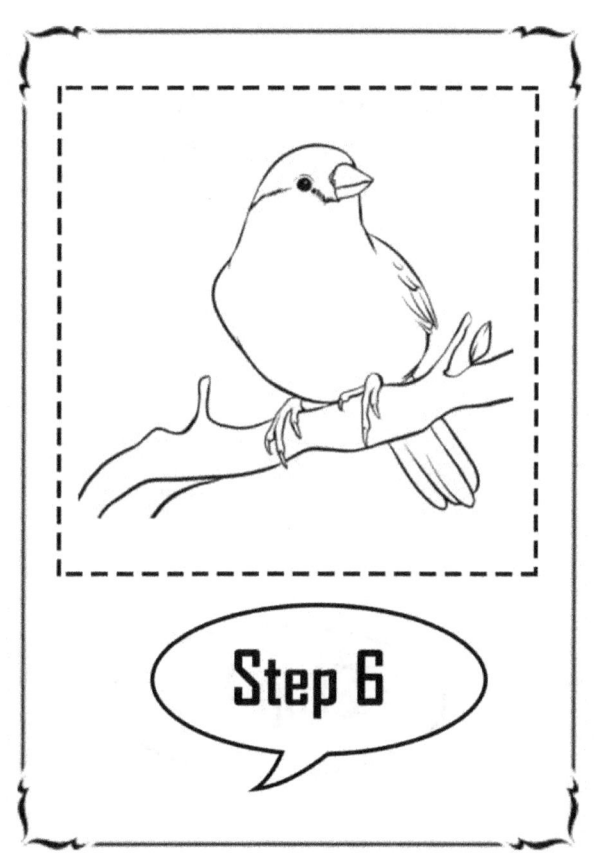

Step 6

Flamingo

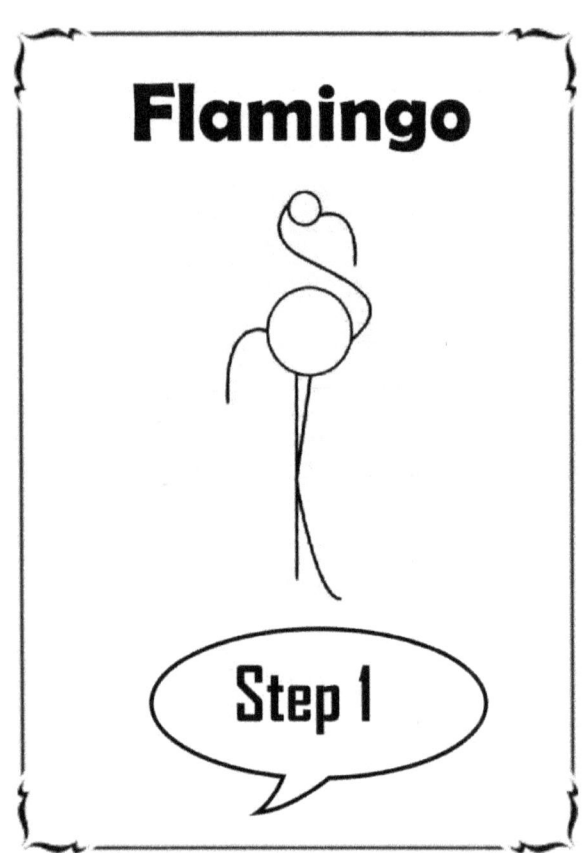

Step 1

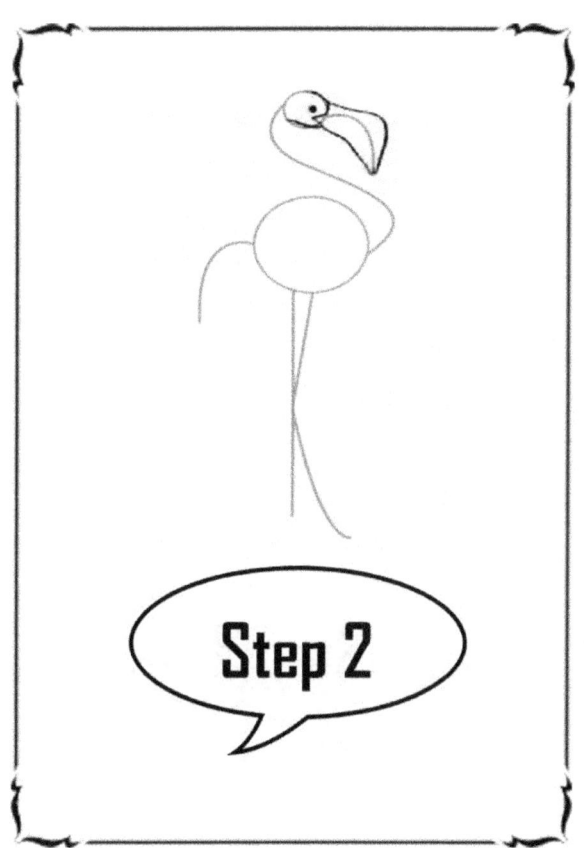

Step 2

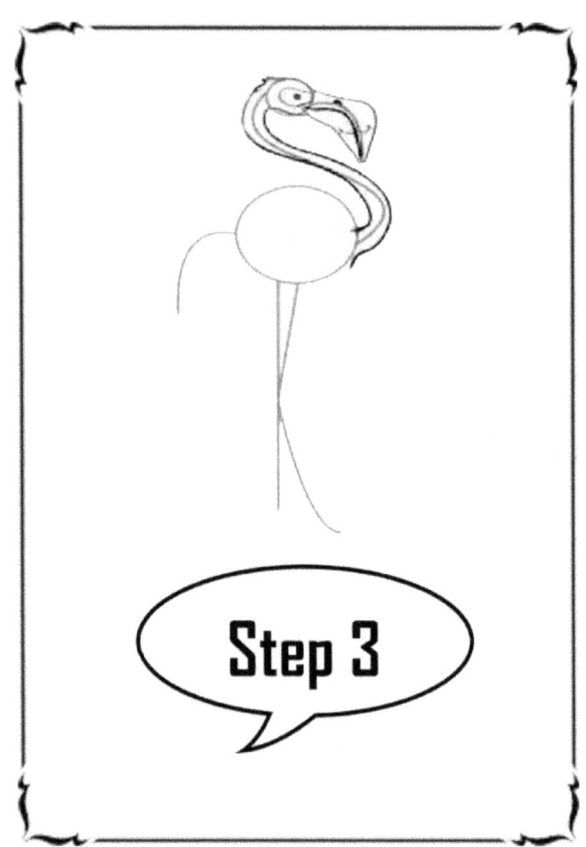

Step 3

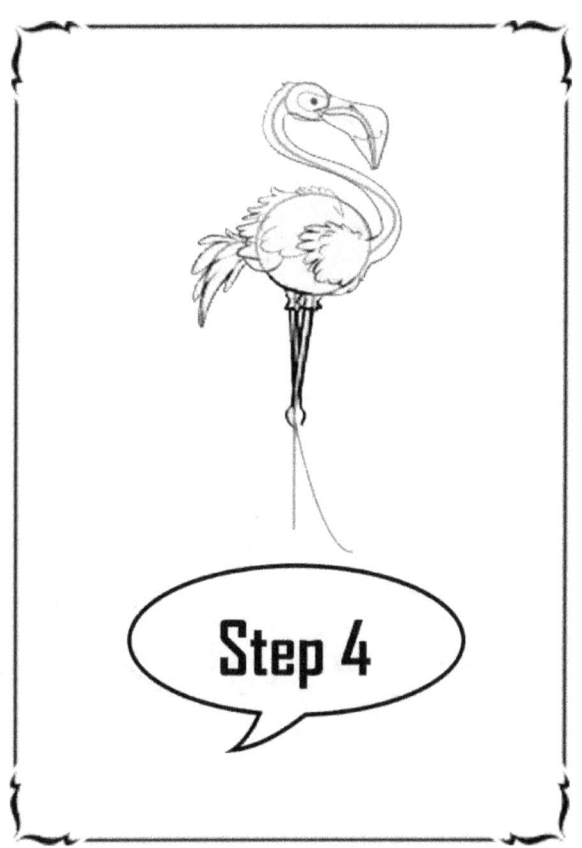

Step 4

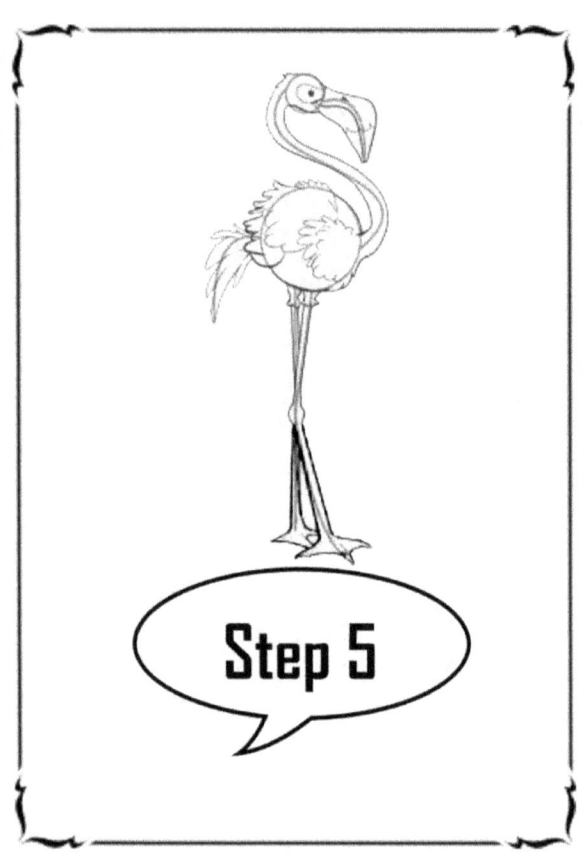

Step 5

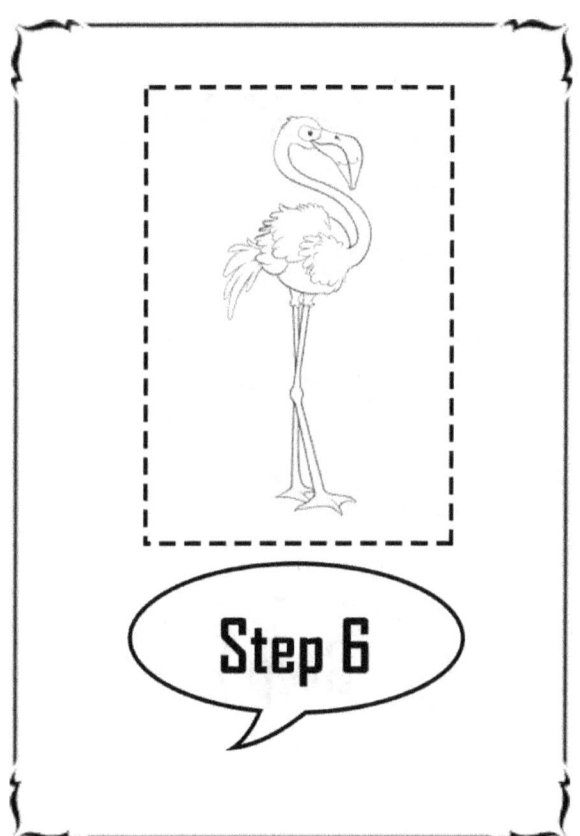

Step 6

Macaw

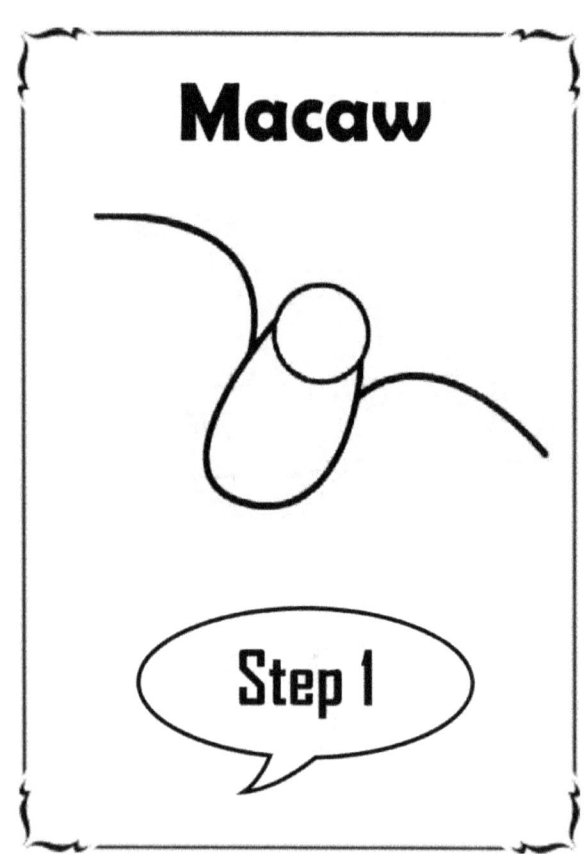

Step 1

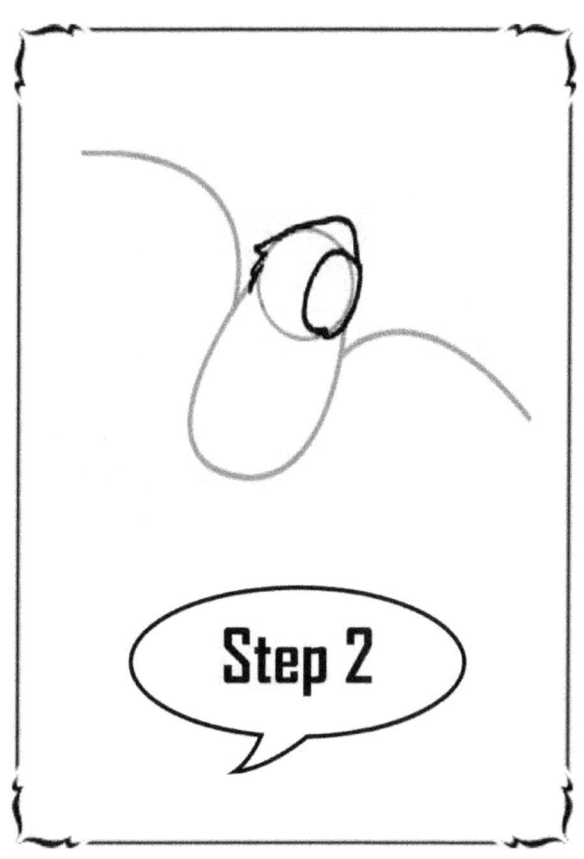

Step 2

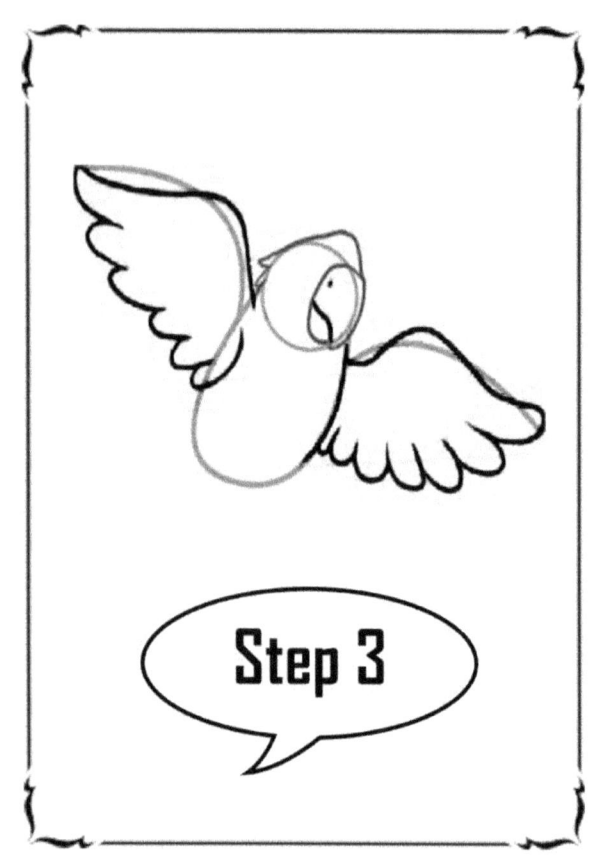

Step 3

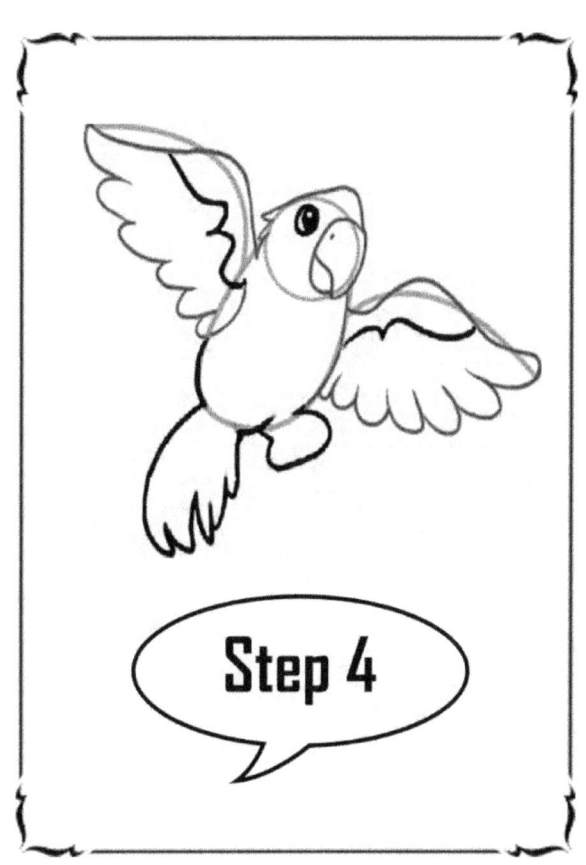

Step 4

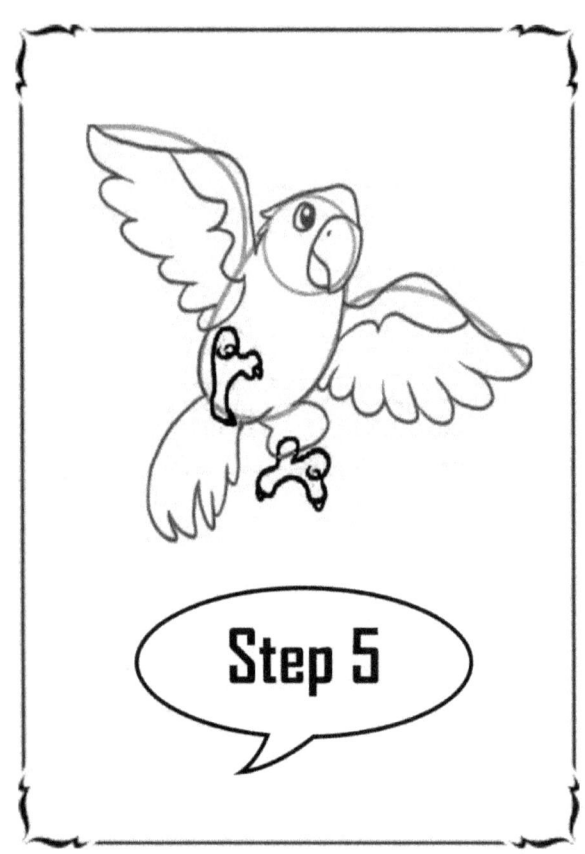

Step 5

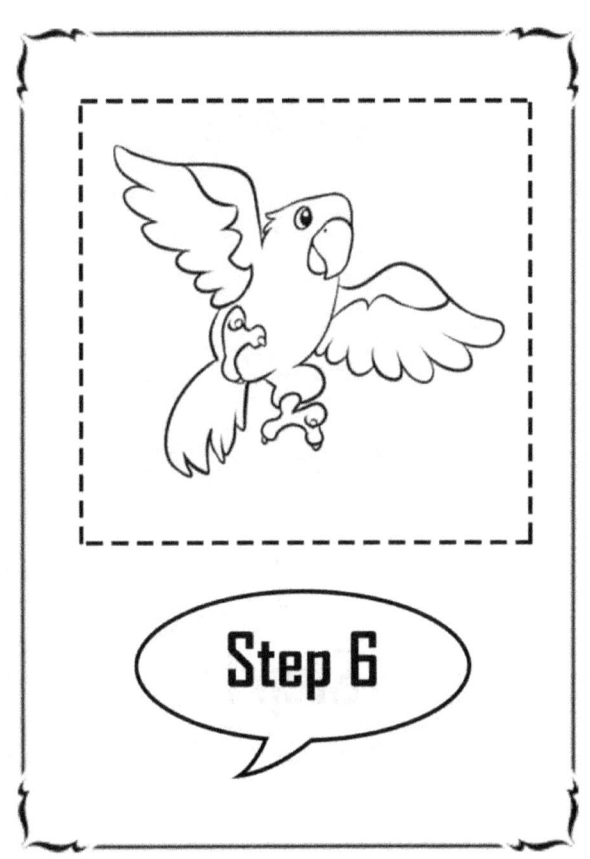

Step 6

Owl

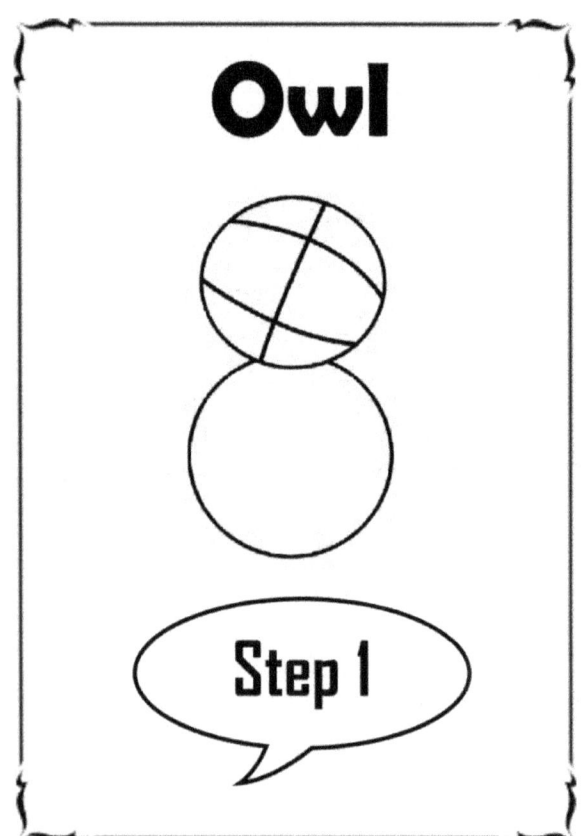

Step 1

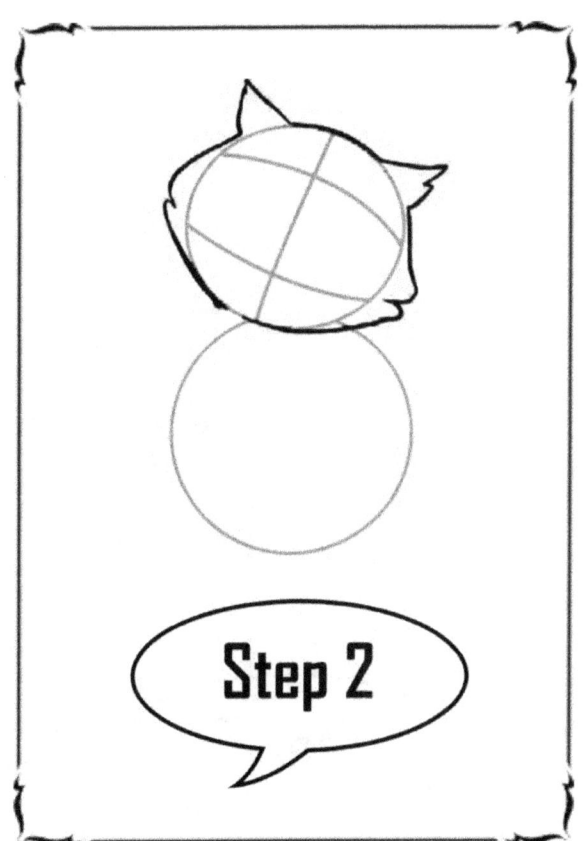

Step 2

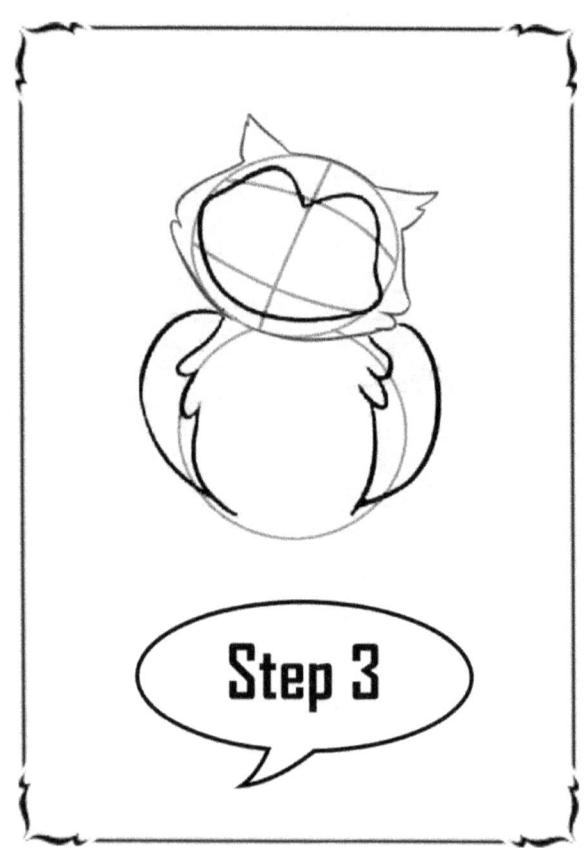

Step 3

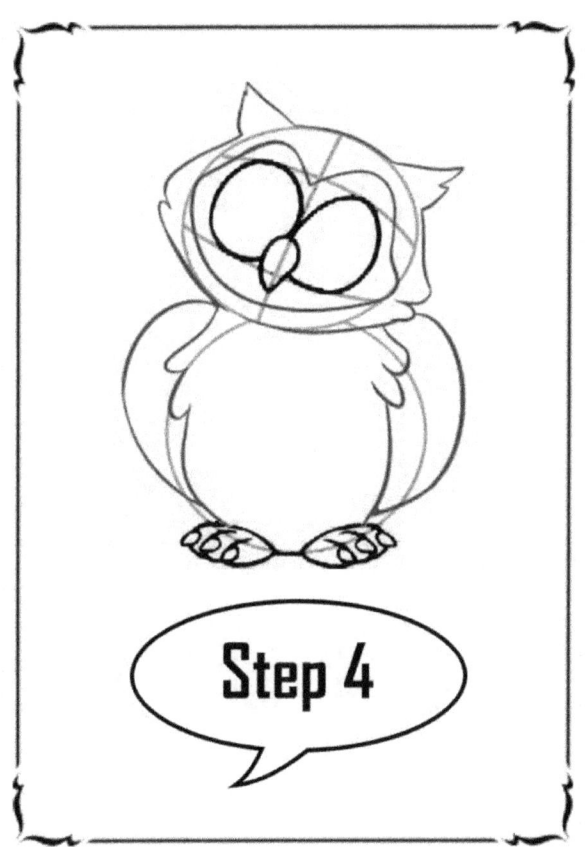

Step 4

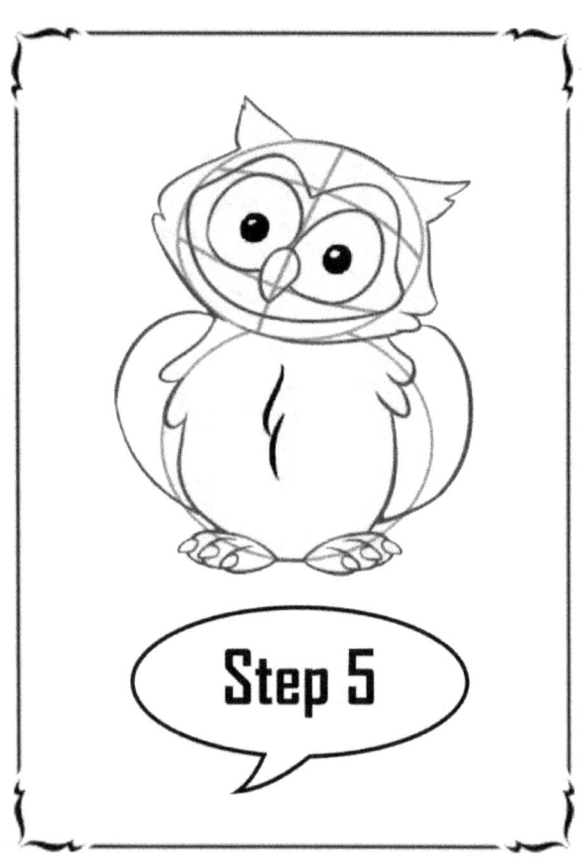

Step 5

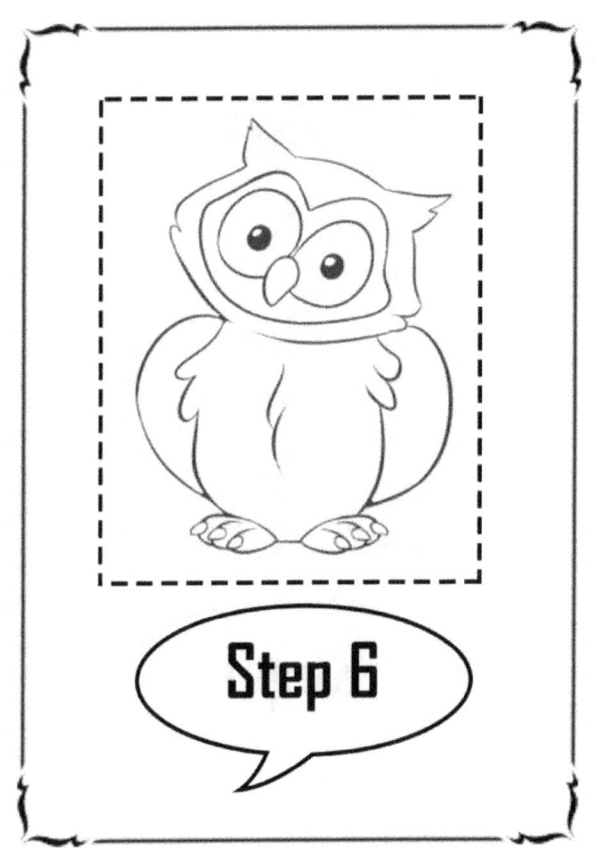

Step 6

Seagull

Step 1

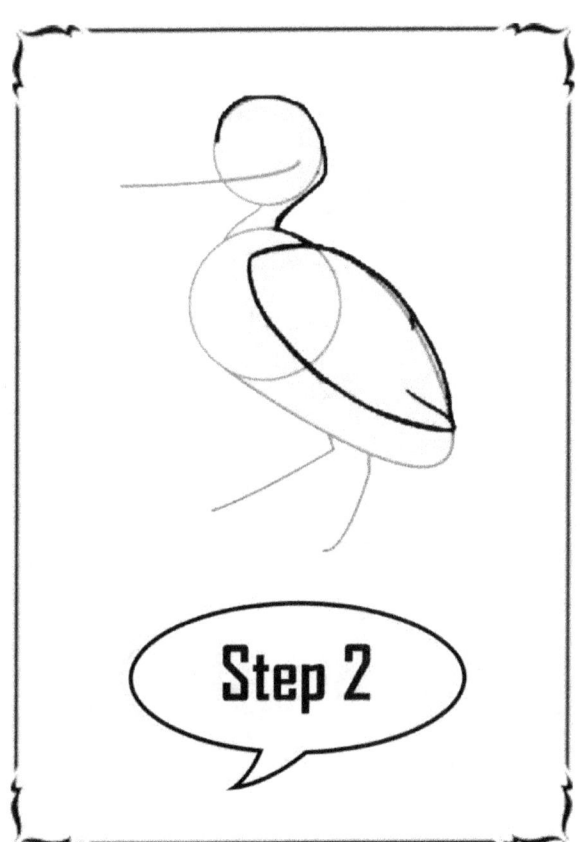

Step 2

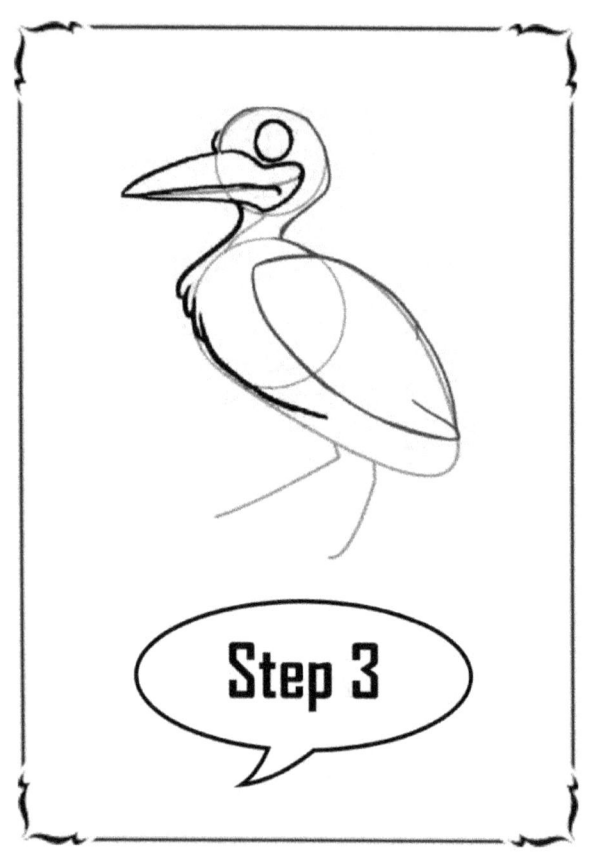

Step 3

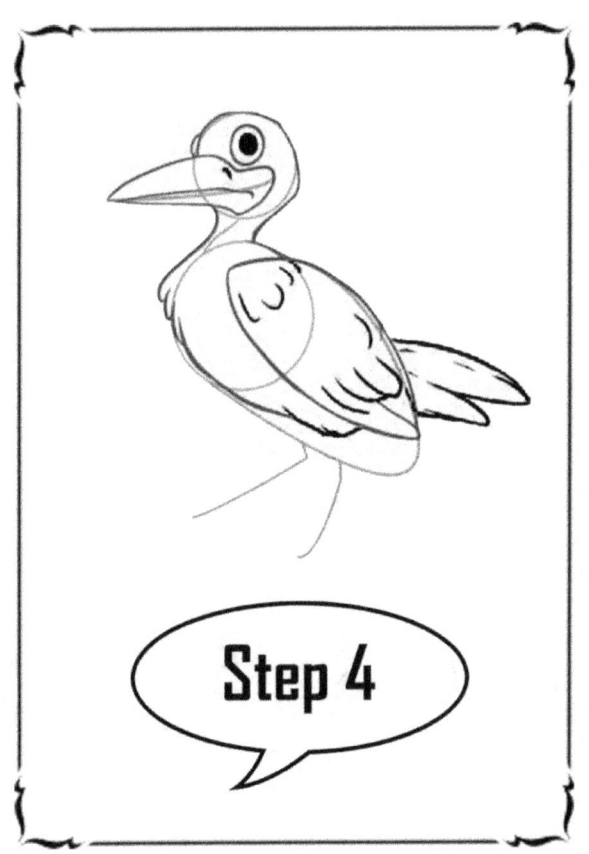

Step 4

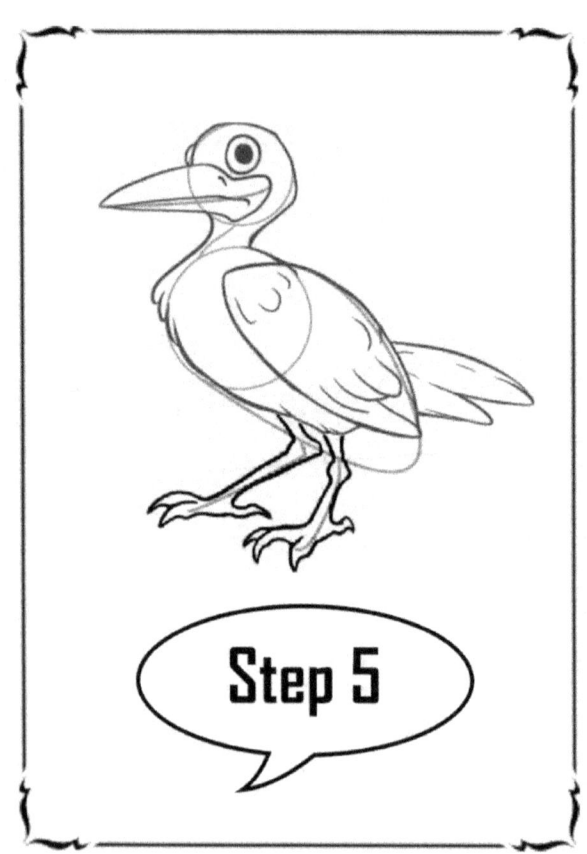

Step 5

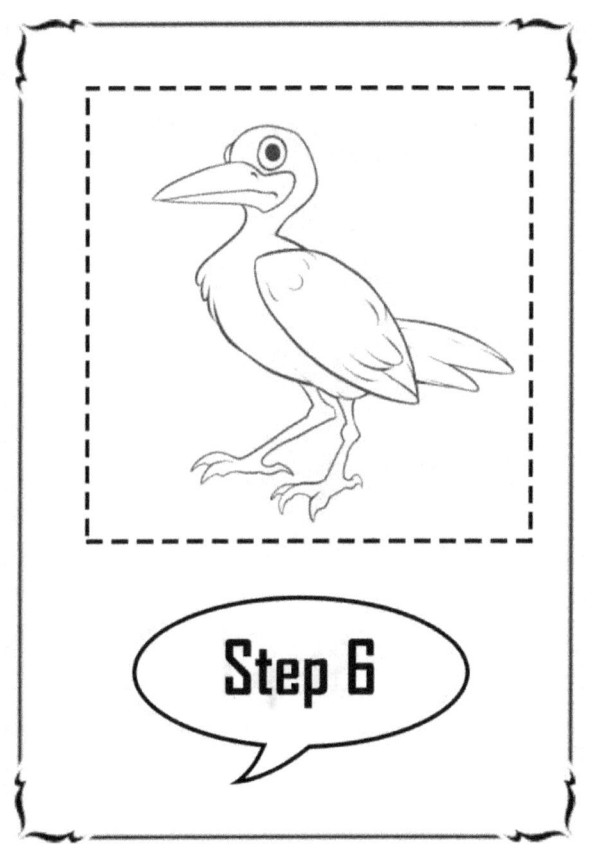

Step 6

Woodpecker

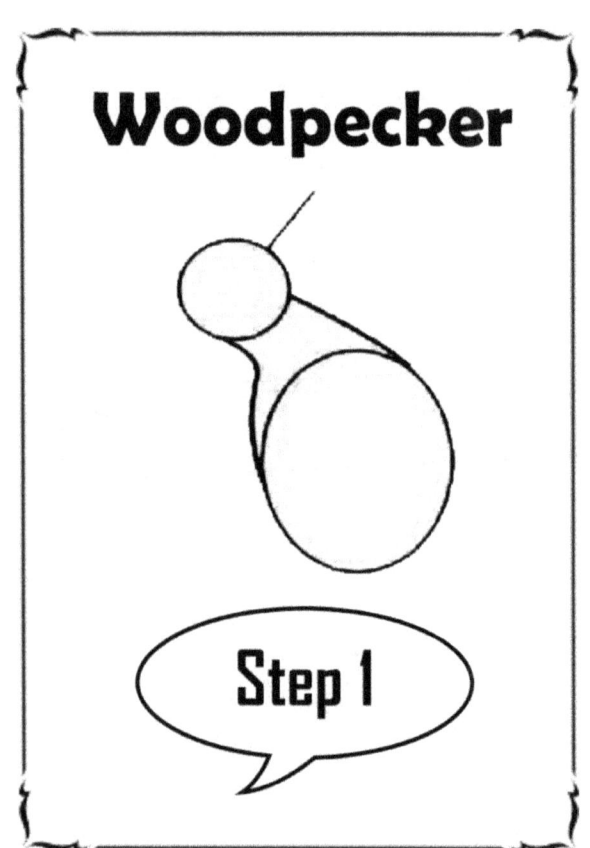

Step 1

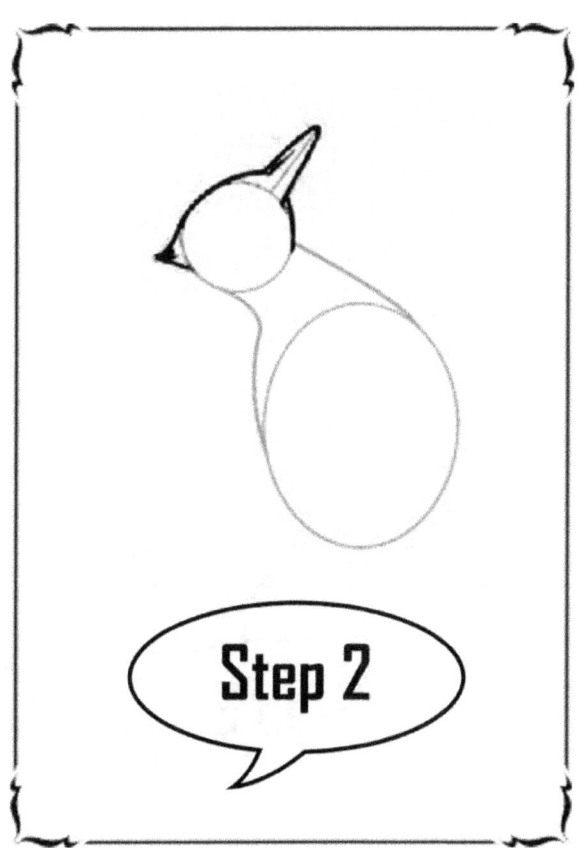

Step 2

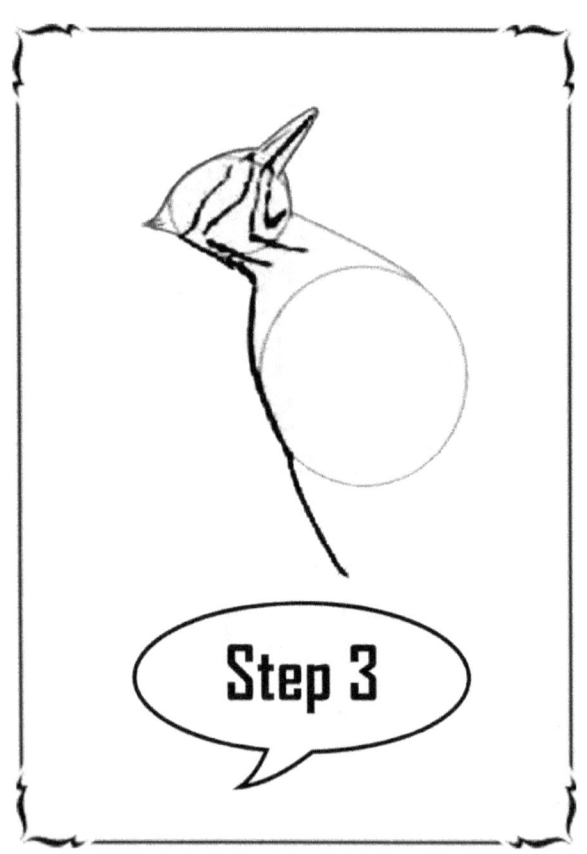

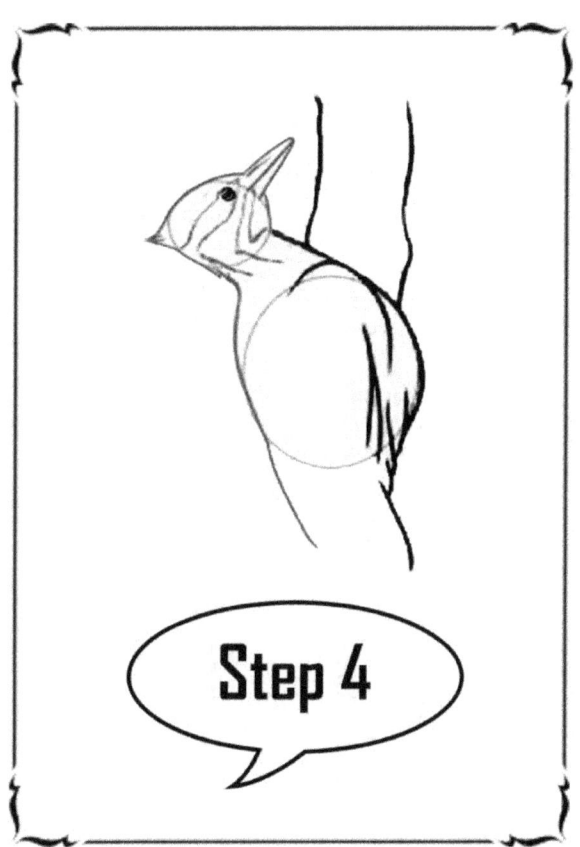

Step 4

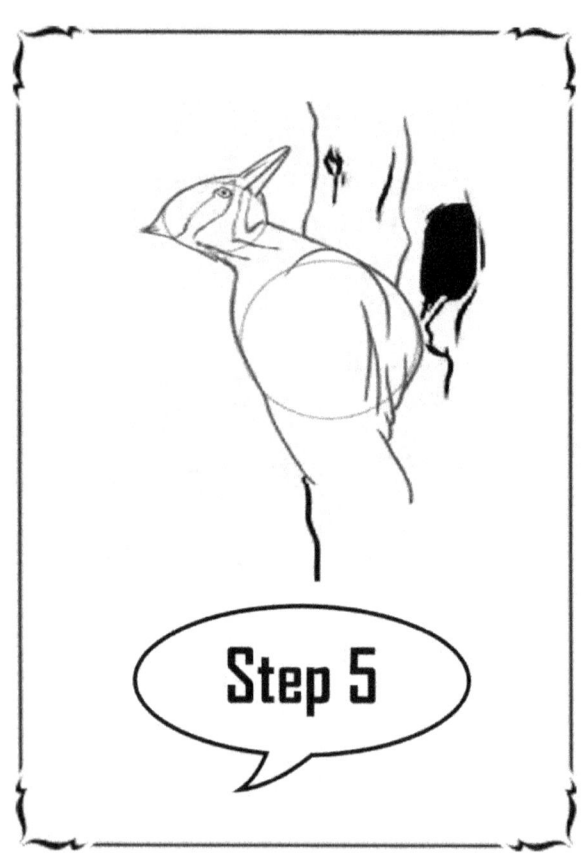

Step 5

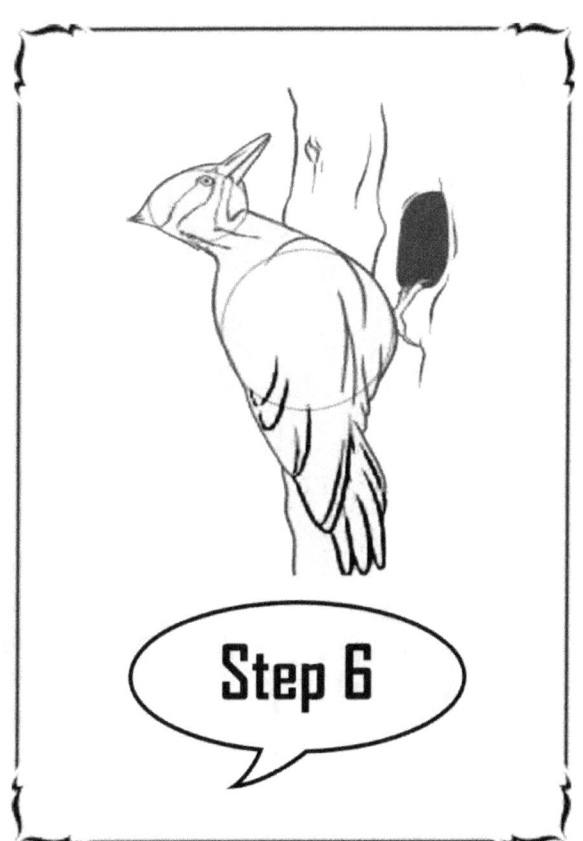

Step 6

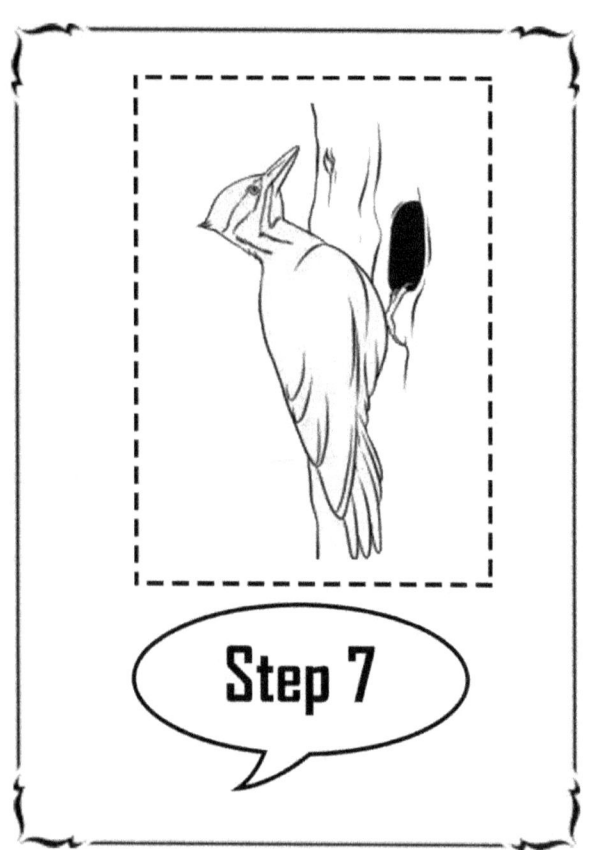

Step 7

Parakeet

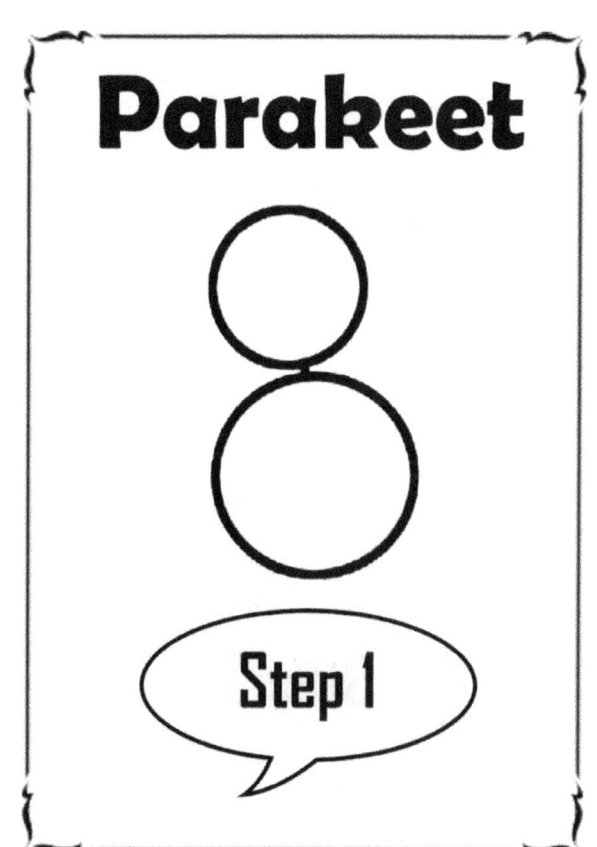

Step 1

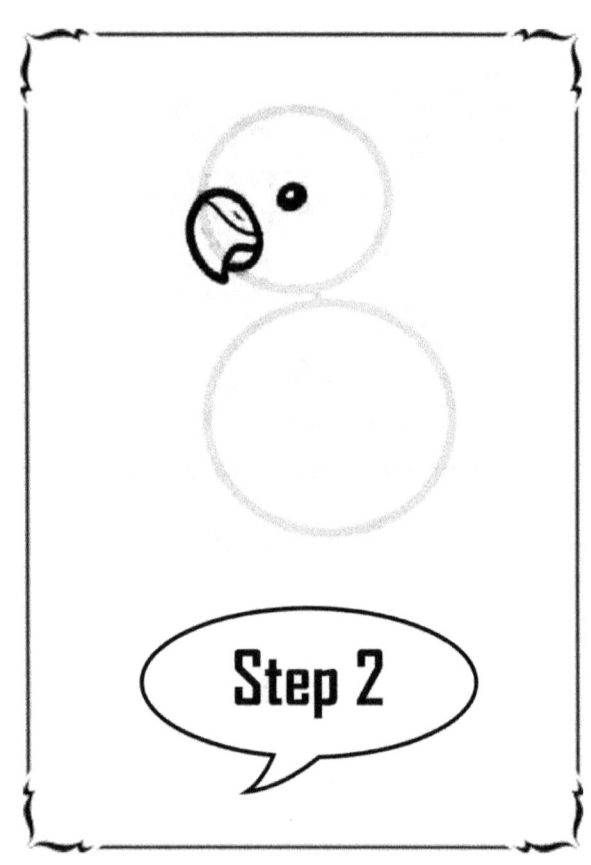

Step 2

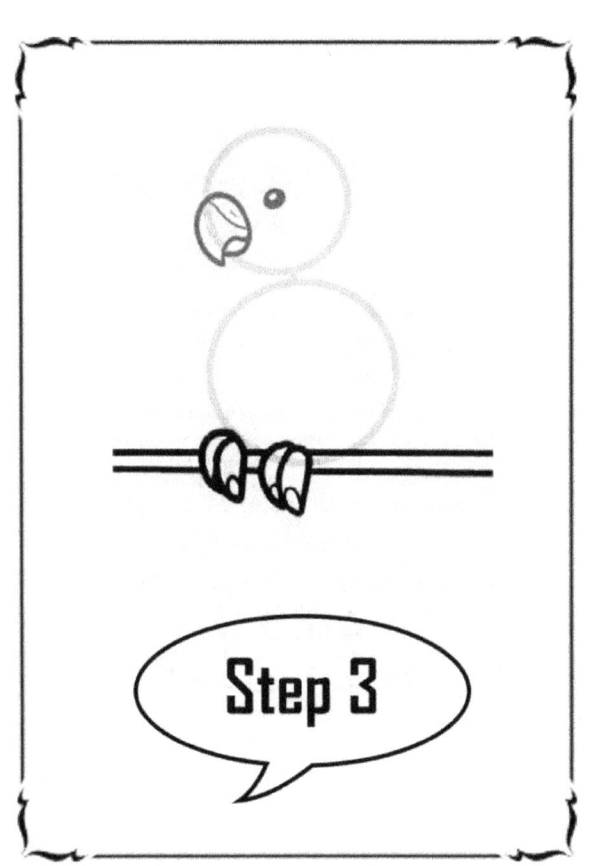

Step 3

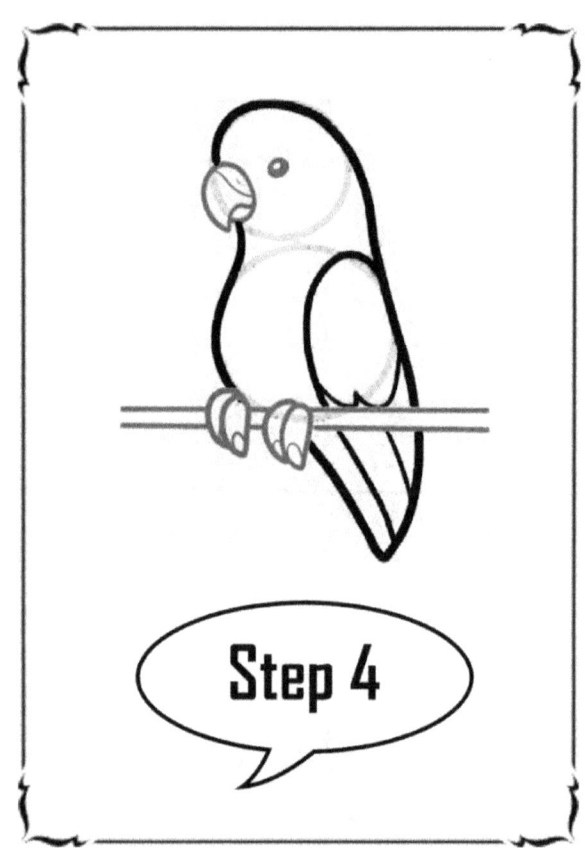

Step 4

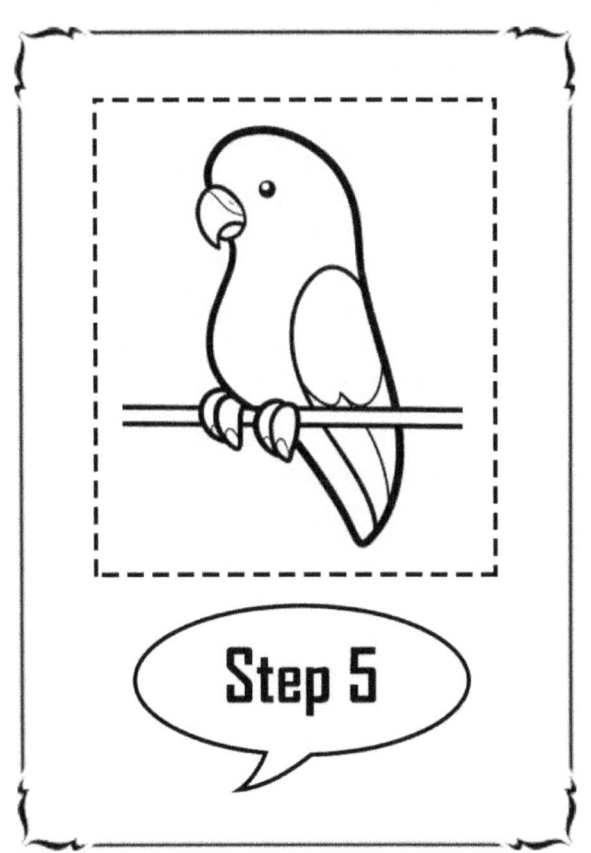

Step 5